Saint Joan of Arc Speaks

Saint Joan of Arc Speaks - Book 1

Published by Abba Books LLC
abbabooksllc@gmail.com

Copyright © 2023 Marie-Josée Thibault

All Rights Reserved

No part of this publication may be reproduced, distributed, or transmitted in any form or by any means, including photocopying, recording, or other electronic or mechanical methods, without the prior written permission of the publisher.

First Edition, 2023
Designed and Edited by Abba Books LLC
ISBN: 979-8-9887805-0-2

Abba Books LLC
34972 Newark Blvd, #441
Newark, CA 94560

www.abbamyfatheriloveyou.com
https://www.facebook.com/AbbaILoveYouBooks/

Thy Peace on Earth must be achieved.

No light, no litany must be spared to honor Thy Grace.

-Saint Paul

Contents

Preface VI	Chap 15 43	Chap 30 87
Chap 1 1	Chap 16 47	Chap 31 89
Chap 2 3	Chap 17 51	Chap 32 91
Chap 3 5	Chap 18 55	Chap 33 93
Chap 4 7	Chap 19 57	Chap 34 95
Chap 5 11	Chap 20 61	Chap 35 97
Chap 6 15	Chap 21 63	Chap 36 99
Chap 7 19	Chap 22 67	Chap 38 105
Chap 8 23	Chap 23 69	Chap 39 109
Chap 9 25	Chap 24 71	Chap 40 113
Chap 10 27	Chap 25 73	Chap 41 117
Chap 11 29	Chap 26 75	Chap 42 119
Chap 12 33	Chap 27 77	Chap 43 123
Chap 13 39	Chap 28 79	Chap 44 125
Chap 14 41	Chap 29 81	Chap 45 129

Preface

Joan of Arc is the saint of courage and strength—the unique qualities she embodied while leading the French Army in the siege of Orléans. She will teach you to be brave and courageous in your daily life. Join us on this wonderful journey!

Marie-Josée

FREE DOWNLOAD

Get your free copy of :
"Saint Padre Pio Speaks: Book 1"
when you sign up to the
author's VIP mailing list!
Get started here:

www.abbamyfatheriloveyou.com

Saint Joan of Arc Speaks

 speak to you from Heaven where I dwell with numerous Saints and Angels in Paradise. I speak to you today through the essence of Saint Paul on earth, Marie-Josée T., to whom I owe my gratitude and my prayers of support and courage.

The Heavenly Father has given me a new mission on earth: the one to lead human troops to the victory of Light over darkness. I am thankful to God for His Love and His Mercy toward you: humans of the earth in growing distress.

Saint Joan of Arc Speaks

Humanity, humanity! I speak to you today with urgency and with intensity: the torments that lie ahead are on a planetary scale and of a tragic extent never seen before in history. Listen to me! My Heart is full of Love and full of Courage and I want to pour forth into each one of your hearts my Divine plenitude! I learned the virtues of courage and solid faith in God during my short journey on earth and I will continue my heroic mission deep within each one of your hearts.

*D*ear humans who inhabit the earth during these end times, I offer myself to your service and I will bring you to victory: your royal entry into the Kingdom of God where I dwell with Christ—my King—and the Angels, as well as the Saints who are alongside me. All here pray for you, for your salvation, for your victory against the dark forces assailing you from all sides, and all here are delighted that my Voice be heard now.

*G*lory be to the Eternal Father, our Benefactor, who allowed this Miracle of communication through the Holy Spirit. May this Message of Courage be heard throughout every heart beating on earth. I make it my Holy prayer…

Saint Joan of Arc Speaks

ear humanity in distress, I am sorrowed, along with the whole Heaven, to notice the deplorable state of your souls. We witness so much neglect, so much Spiritual laziness, so much materialism! The Eternal Father, our Father Creator of all, is deeply offended by this.

It is now my duty to command you in the inner battle taking place in your hearts—each one of you. I shall impart onto you the courage, perseverance, and hope necessary for your victory over the dark world of the ego that is overwhelming you. At the battle! Now! Follow me! Now! May your soul be claimed by the Angels of God and not the soldiers of the devil at the moment of passage that is death! Amen.

Saint Joan of Arc Speaks

4

ear humanity that I love so much, remember me! The injustices, the cruelties, the blasphemies and the attacks I endured during my journey on earth as Joan of Arc were horrible! I was a brave girl—albeit naive—totally devoted to Christ Jesus, my King, whom I wanted to serve with my life, my soul, my heart. So many inner conflicts! Such confusion in my thoughts! Such doubts invaded me!

However, an extraordinary transformation took place in my heart at Rouen in 1431 when I was imprisoned. I saw Christ Jesus with my own eyes, I heard Him speak to me directly, and He took me in His Arms! This Miracle took place in my cell, in secret, out of sight or hearing of anyone.

Christ Jesus, my Savior and my God, visited me, healed me, and He changed my human heart into a Divine Heart by His Celestial Love and Grace. I was in a state of Mystical rapture and incredible cosmic clarity without compare. How much Love in my Heart! How much strength in my body! How much determination in my will!

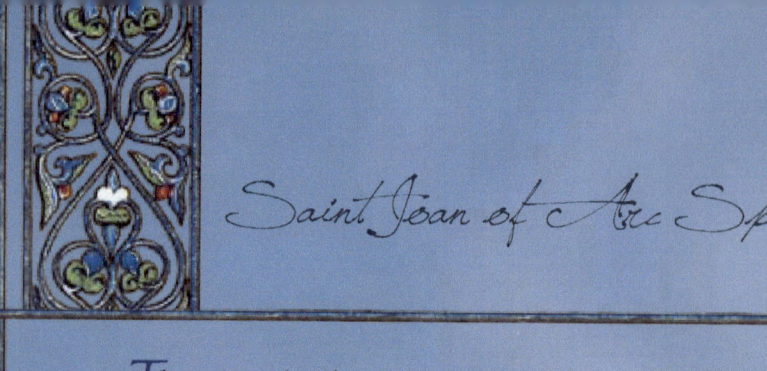

Saint Joan of Arc Speaks

That is why I wish to speak to you today! My Message is this: be firm in your faith, be courageous in your actions, be focused in your vision, and pray! Pray! Pray!

Christ Jesus, the King of Heaven and earth, is always with you, and He will manifest Himself in your life if you ask Him! Your merits add up every day and bring you closer to Him continuously… Pray! Pray! Pray! And you will be saved by Christ Jesus Himself! Amen!

Saint Joan of Arc Speaks

 y children of a promised earth, I speak to you from Heaven, yet, I am very close to you; at this very moment I am speaking to you! The Saints in Paradise, the Angels of God, Christ Jesus our Lord and our King, our Blessed Mother, the Holy Spirit and the Eternal Father, all occupying the Kingdom of Heaven, are here, very much near you—in your heart.

The Energetic dimensions that are surrounding you and that fabricate your body are full of life, of Divine inhabitants like me, who move freely, rushing to the slightest call, and capable of interceding on your behalf to obtain miracles and wishes fulfilled.

Since my physical death in 1431, and my intact passage into the Kingdom of God, I have worked tirelessly for the people of the earth. Wars and military battles of our humanity are well-known to me, for I have participated in them as a Source of fortitude, courage, and determination, toward the righteous souls guided by the Holy Spirit.

Saint Joan of Arc Speaks

My Divine assistance has enabled the resolution of many conflicts that have disturbed the peace of mankind, and this at the world level as easily as at the individual level—throughout the whole earth and during all these years.

I know the human heart; I know the tricks and perfidies of the tenebrous soldiers, and I know the Law of God my Creator. I am able to influence your thoughts, to inspire strategies, and to boost the vital Energy of your physical body if necessary, through the operations of the Holy Spirit. No matter if you call me… I am always there, and I assist you in your struggles, whatever they may be.

And now, thanks to this book blessed by God, I am brimming with Celestial Powers for you, for Christ Jesus has decided so toward you—and my gratitude to Him is endless.

Holy, Holy, Holy Lord God of Hosts. Heaven and earth are full of Your Glory: Hosanna in the Highest. Blessed is he who comes in the Name of the Lord: Hosanna in the Highest. Amen.

Saint Joan of Arc Speaks

y dear children of the suffering earth, where will you take refuge when the end times strike the entire planet? In your houses? In the government shelters? With the military forces?

No physical structure whatsoever will protect you. For the human flesh is of little value in the Eyes of our Father of all—God Almighty. Our Father Sovereign is primarily concerned with the state of your soul before He is preoccupied with your corporeal envelope. Your soul is invested with His Energy; your soul is in His Image and Likeness.

However, too many souls are soiled on this earth of disgrace, therefore God's Plan of Salvation includes a deep and complete cleansing and purification of all souls who inhabit the earth. The physical body, therefore, shall be preserved, only if the soul that lives therein is pure enough to see God.

Saint Joan of Arc Speaks

And if not, the body will be destroyed and the soiled soul will have to undergo an unparalleled Energetic transformation of Divine nature, so that one day, all souls that circulate in all the dimensions of the Creation are worthy of God and as Beautiful as God.

Alleluia! Alleluia! Alleluia! May all the souls sing the praises of God the Father, our Creator and our Sovereign! Amen!

Saint Joan of Arc Speaks

7

My beloved children, do not be swayed by the voices and clamors of today's society that does not suspect anything. Nothing that you see around you will survive the events that lie ahead—no matter the audacity of my words and the inconceivability of such a global catastrophe.

I say unto you, I say unto you verily, the world as you know it shall be no more.

God's Plan of Salvation is Powerful. It is extraordinarily Powerful; it is inevitably Powerful. Nothing, absolutely nothing, can stop God's Plan of Salvation, for everything, absolutely everything, must change on earth.

The Father wishes the Cosmic Transformation of His Creation, through all the dimensions that He Himself generated, so that all darkness gives way to the Light, the Light of Christ, our Lord Jesus Christ, His Only and Glorious Son, Who will emerge as King Sovereign over everything and visible everywhere...shortly.

Alleluia! Alleluia! Alleluia! Blessed is he who comes in the Name of the Lord. Amen. So be it.

Glory be to the Eternal Father, our Benefactor, who allowed this miracle of communication through the Holy Spirit. May this message of courage be heard throughout every heart beating on earth.

Saint Joan of Arc
(1412-1431)

I make it my holy prayer...

Saint Joan of Arc Speaks

y dear children of the earth, my Might to act in your lives is true and impressive: I have the Power to overcome obstacles for your benefit; I have the ability to influence your thinking and that of individuals involved with you. I am in a strategic position to negotiate on your behalf before the Father Creator, through Gifts of Miracles that Heaven share for you—these Gifts that have been won by the Holy Cross and the Sacred Wounds of our Lord Jesus Christ, our Savior and our King.

My earthly life as Joan of Arc enabled me to develop and obtain the Gifts of the Holy Spirit, and I hasten to teach you in detail the profound principles of the operations of the Holy Spirit. For the Holy Spirit—truly God the Holy Spirit—loves you, helps you and supports you at every moment of your life, more than you can imagine.

Alleluia! Alleluia! Alleluia! Blessed is he who prays to the Holy Spirit, God of Love of the Holy Trinity! Amen!

Saint Joan of Arc Speaks

y dear children of the earth in peril, listen carefully: the Holy Spirit is with you, with each one of you—continually. The Holy Spirit, God the Holy Spirit, is everywhere, through everything, and at all times present in the known universe of men.

God the Holy Spirit—Very Powerful God the Holy Spirit—reveals to us the fundamental principles at the basis of Christic Teaching through His transcendent operations proceeding constantly in the Energetic dimensions of the cosmos. His revelations are always true, direct and simple, and are conducted in order to establish in mankind a deep comprehension and a progressive clarification of the essential and important Mysteries of the Creation.

For the Holy Spirit knows everything, sees everything, and hears everything, such as the rest of the Holy Trinity, with Who He interacts constantly in order to fulfill the Will of the Father, with Divine and Infinite Perfection. For the Holy Spirit is Love, tangible Love touching you, serene Love pacifying you, Spiritual Love healing you of anything.

Alleluia! Alleluia! Alleluia! Blessed is he who prays to the Holy Spirit every day, for the Sacred Mysteries of the universe shall be revealed to him! Amen!

Saint Joan of Arc Speaks

My children, my children: time is running out. Convert today to Christ Jesus, my Lord and my Savior, to Whom I owe everything.

When I was burned at the stake on May 30, 1431, in a state of shock and extreme fright, I was saved in the middle of the flames by Christ Jesus Himself! He swiftly and gently removed me from the flames that had started to tear at my flesh. More Beautiful than an Angel, more radiant than the sun, I was as equally dazzled by His Heart, beating in Infinite Love, which was visible through His Holy Chest. Such wonder! Such joy! Such relief!

My life on earth was crowned by my final liberation into the Arms of my Savior and my God! Supreme and Ineffable Benediction from Heaven! Amen!

Alleluia! Alleluia! Alleluia! I pray that you are also received into the majestic Arms of my King, the Lord Jesus, at the outcome of the passage that is death. I love you, from Saint Joan of Arc. Amen.

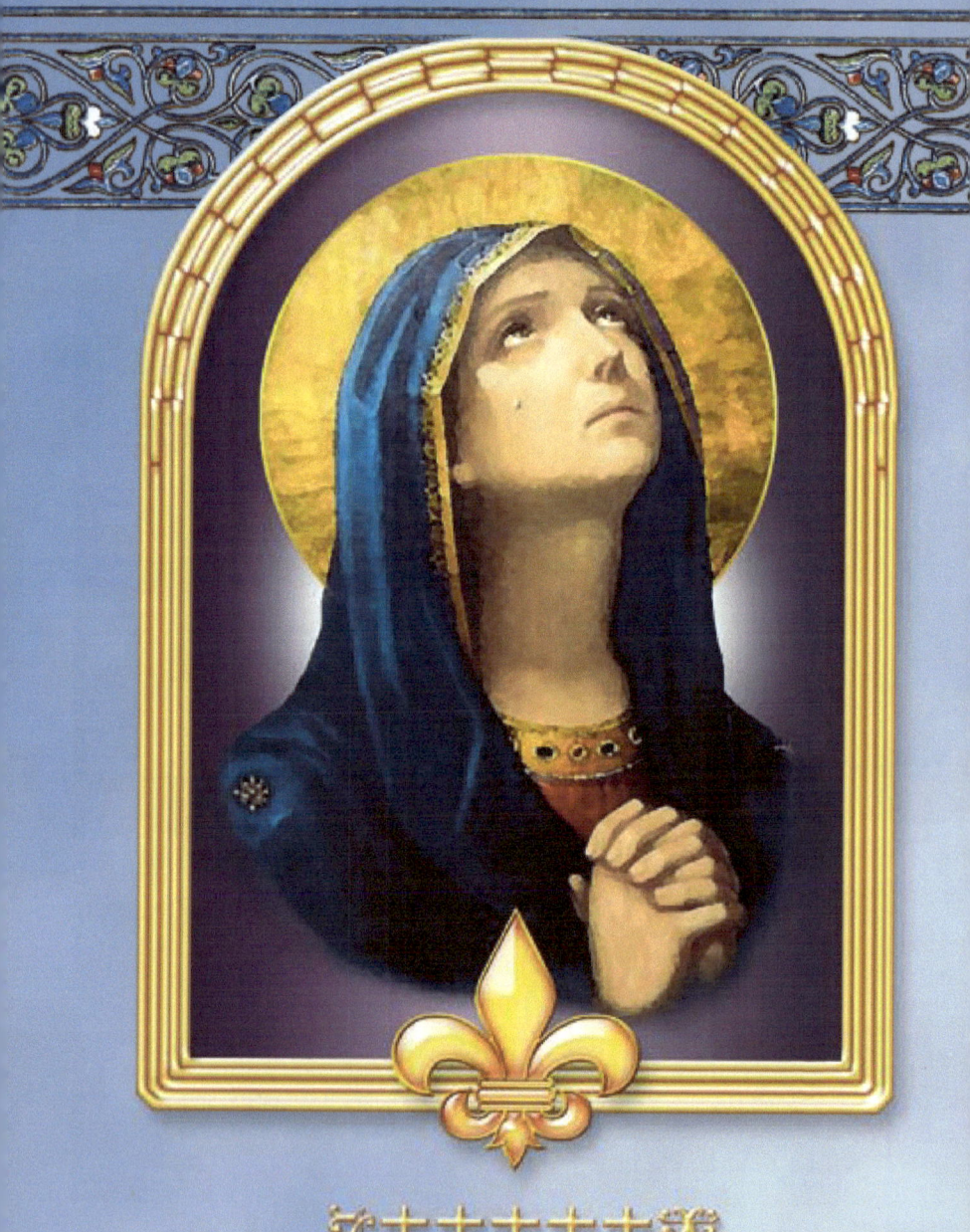

Saint Joan of Arc Speaks

II

y dear children, I am pleased to see efforts displayed in order to defeat the psychological enemy that is the ego. However, one must not interrupt this process of observation of the dark and negative forces invading your intellect and your heart.

One must act briskly, grasping a dark thought (not of Christ) or a dark emotion (not of Christ) and isolate it within your inner psychological world, observing it without attachment and without judgment, becoming aware that this thought or emotion is a mistake and does not belong to you, and use your will to transform yourself in order to actively eliminate this defect or bad habit—this ego.

Our personal Divine Mother assists us in this process of conscious transformation of our hearts. One must act within oneself firmly, with uprightness, and with the attention of the awakened Consciousness. Your psychological errors—collectively called the ego—are manipulated and amplified by the forces of evil in order to sabotage your life and weaken your faith in Jesus the Christ.

Saint Joan of Arc Speaks

This process of elimination of the ego takes place constantly in the psychological world of the essence who wishes to reconcile with its own Spiritual reality. For with each victory against a little aggregate of darkness that fades away and disappears is earned as much light that was hidden and that emerges from the darkness and floods the soul. Thus, the soul awakens gradually, by virtue of this Divine Light issued from the deep understanding of your inner dynamic, gradually restored therein.

I wish to assist you in the matter of such inner struggle—the universal and archetypal battle taking place between the dark forces and the White Forces, between the ego and the Consciousness, between the tenebrous forces of the devil and the Divine Powers of God.

Alleluia! Alleluia! Alleluia! Blessed is the essence who observes itself with vigilance and takes the decision to fight satan—wherever he is and whatever he does, inside and outside—in the Name of Christ Jesus! Amen!

Saint Joan of Arc Speaks

y dear children, I speak to you from above, from the Kingdom of Heaven awaiting you, but I work with you, right next to you. When you call for my help, I rush to meet you, and I get very close to you, right in front of your physical body.

I know it is difficult for you to conceive such proximity and such connection between the dimensions. Nevertheless, it is the truth! This is why, we, the inhabitants of Paradise, are in a position to help you immediately, and why we are so intimate in your life.

Verily, verily I say unto you, he who prays to the Eternal Father and asks for the intercession of the Saints in Paradise, in the Name of Christ Jesus, our Savior and our God, truly is equipped with a miraculous and thundering Force before the Father.

Many times a day, simply say: "Saint Joan of Arc, intercede for me, before God the Father, for the obtention of [requested favor], by virtue of your Gift of Strength and Courage, through the Sacred Wounds of our Lord Christ Jesus and the Immaculate Heart of Mary. Amen."

Saint Joan of Arc Speaks

For the Father Almighty is most sensitive to requests from the Saints in Paradise, as they have obtained their Sanctification by virtue of the imitation of Christ, His Only Son. Henceforth, consequently, each of the Saints in Paradise has also become a Christ; whereas His Son, Christ Jesus, is Christ the King—the most elevated Being of the Creation—for He is One with God and the Holy Spirit within the Holy Trinity.

Alleluia! Alleluia! Alleluia! Blessed is he who communes with the Saints in Paradise, for their Energetic Presence extends like a miraculous Arc between your essence on earth and the Father Most High Who loves us all! Amen. Alleluia!

I will help you acquire the graces of strength and courage ~ Joan

Saint Joan of Arc Speaks

y dear children of the earth, I say unto you, I say unto you verily, follow my example. I was persecuted, I was betrayed, I was physically ill-treated; I had to face great danger on several levels in order to fulfill the mission given to me and to give Glory to my King of Heaven, the Lord Jesus Christ.

Be not afraid! Your bravery and your courage are carefully noted and supported by a Celestial Army of amplitude and proportions that you cannot suspect seen from below. The aches and pains that come across are all the more gestures of love and obedience toward our Sovereign God, our Lord, who has suffered more than any other man of this humanity.

If you wish one day to enter the Kingdom of Heaven, you must imitate Christ Jesus in all aspects taught by the Church, as well as by the other messengers of His Teaching through the ages—including Marie-Josée T., the one taking this dictation at this time. For the Words of Christ and the Words of the Saints in Paradise who have also become Christ are the Way, the Truth, and the Life.

Alleluia! Alleluia! Alleluia! Blessed is he who comes in the Name of the Lord, for with Him, is the Way, the Truth, and the Life. Amen.

Saint Joan of Arc Speaks

14

y dear children of the earth, I will be clear here: do not remain in the collective incredulity and weakness that society is trying to establish in order to operate according to its political dogmas. Wake up!

Do you not see the major collective issues that make you dependent on money and a façade of prestige desired by all? Do you not see the global manipulation rewarding those supposedly elected to power by stripping from the masses below?

I say unto you, I say unto you verily: God the Father does not tolerate this structure in place and the tenebrous forces supporting it. For the end times have been brought about as a result of evil spirits roaming around humanity in order to make it collapse.

Alleluia! Alleluia! Alleluia! Blessed be the righteous and virtuous heart, for God the Eternal Father will be equally righteous and virtuous toward him! Amen! So be it.

Saint Joan of Arc Speaks

y dear children, listen to me, for my Words are Holy and Sacred. I am Saint Joan of Arc and I am a messenger of God Almighty. I was granted permission to speak to you personally for I have prayed before God the Father for a long time.

Why? Because the planetary disasters that lie ahead are atrocious. However, the struggle for survival is to take place not in the bleak future that is upon us, but rather right now. The battle of which I speak, the real battle that confronts you, is the one that is played between the Light and the darkness that lie within you.

When I speak of your Light, I refer to your Consciousness, this Eternal Spark that derives from your Divine Father, and who is the Eternal and Divine part of your reality—also known as your essence or soul. When I speak of your darkness, I refer to the ego, the obscure and confusing part of your personality. Your Consciousness wishes to join with God and your ego wishes to join with satan.

That is, in a few words, the battle taking place at any given moment within your psychological world: in your intellect through your thoughts and in your heart through your emotions.

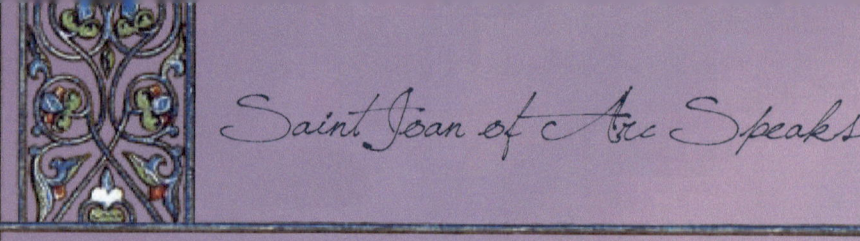
Saint Joan of Arc Speaks

I intervene at this level, at once psychological and Mystical, in order to clarify the way forward—that is to say, the way of Christ—and to strengthen you in your decisive and victorious steps.

*F*or your victory vis-à-vis satan is accomplished now, today, through the small events of everyday life, in order to prepare the armor of protection that you will need during tomorrow's disasters. Victory is at hand now—and Eternally.

*A*lleluia! Alleluia! Alleluia! Blessed is he who invokes the Sacred Name of Saint Joan of Arc before God, for promised victory is theirs! Amen. Alleluia!

Saint Joan of Arc Speaks

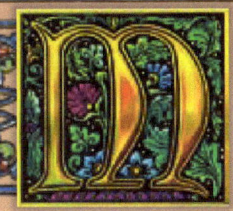y children, I am powerful, for Christ Jesus, my Lord and my God, made me this way. I make it my continual prayer: ask Him to make you powerful as well, capable of fundamental works for the sake of humanity, and beaming with Divine and Transcendent Energy in order to accomplish your mission with perfection.

For your mission is equally as unique and equally as important as the mission I was given in 1429, according to the perspective of God the Father Who loves us all equally and completely.

Christ Jesus can do everything for you from one end of the spectrum of miracles to the other, of which you are dreaming—and far beyond. For Christ Jesus is the Master of the world. Amen. Alleluia!

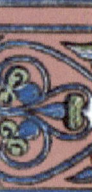

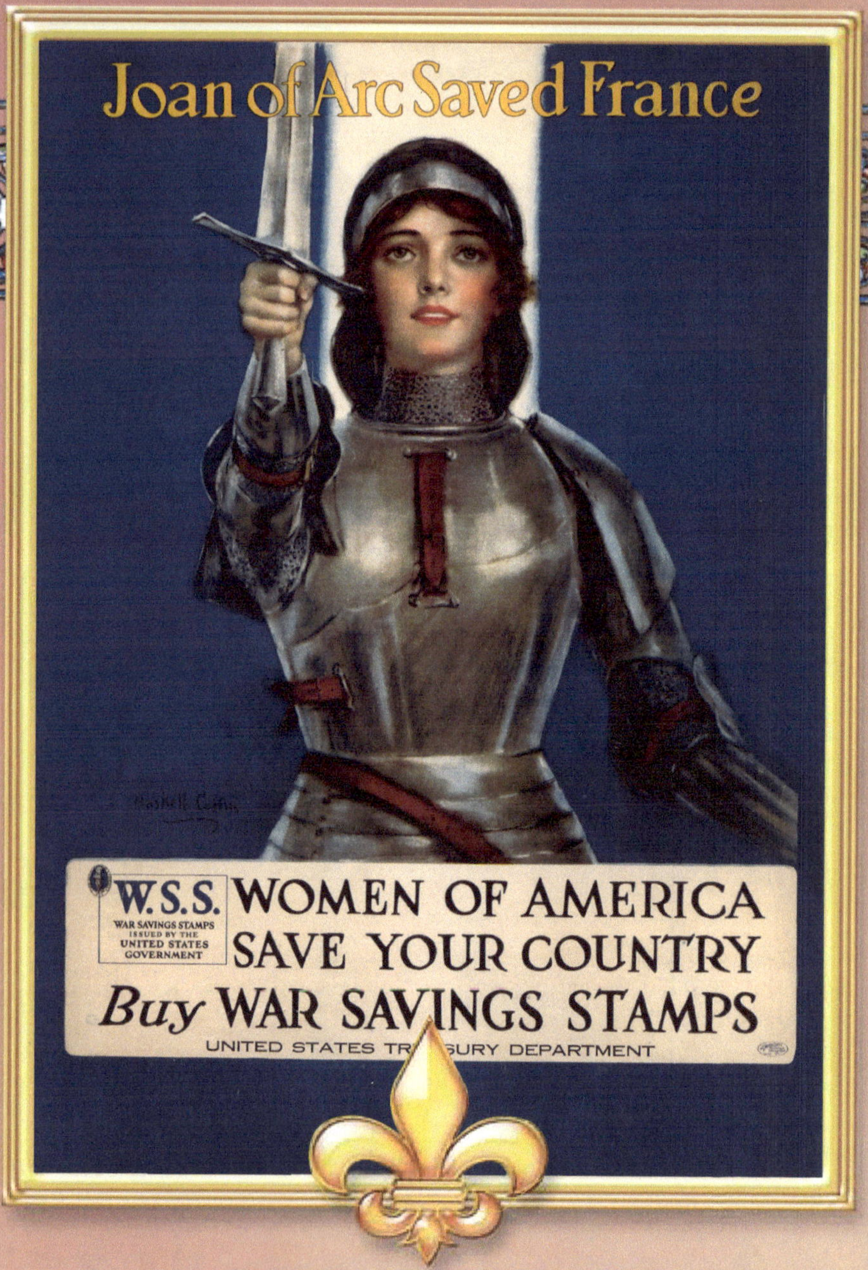
Joan of Arc Saved France
W.S.S.
WAR SAVINGS STAMPS
ISSUED BY THE
UNITED STATES
GOVERNMENT
WOMEN OF AMERICA
SAVE YOUR COUNTRY
Buy WAR SAVINGS STAMPS
UNITED STATES TR SURY DEPARTMENT

Saint Joan of Arc Speaks

 y children, my children, remain careful in your actions and remain vigilant in your thoughts. Do not let the enemy slip through your daily routine by temptations, neglect, and even subtle weariness.

I say unto you, I say unto you verily, stand like a soldier in the psychological battle unfolding constantly in your inner world. Practice the following observations: Am I in a state of anger? Vanity? Resentment? Jealousy? And why? Or am I in a state of charity? Humility? Love and forgiveness? And why?

Make the decision to transform your negative emotions into positive emotions. Stand up and say No to toxic emotions in your life! Take your sword and cut the strings of dependence that are tying you to the past and that contain so much error and false conditioning! Walk with determination in the territory of temptation (marital difficulties, workplace disputes, bitter but necessary conversations) and once and for all, walk in righteousness, in truth, in generosity, in love and forgiveness!

Saint Joan of Arc Speaks

Be victorious in the battle that you are leading within yourself! That is the fundamental key to your victory against the enemy, for the enemy is not outside, but it is rather hidden within you! The enemy is the ego, the collection of errors of your personality, the negative elements invading you, and the weaknesses utilized by the demon to make you fall.

Alleluia! Alleluia! Alleluia! Blessed be the soldier who is preparing for battle, for he deserves the intercession of Saint Joan of Arc! Let us pray before God the Father for obtaining the strength and courage needed to win the inner battle of your life, so that you can offer to God Almighty your purified and victorious soul, inundated with the Glory of Christ Jesus our Lord and Savior! Amen! So be it.

Saint Joan of Arc Speaks

y children, listen to me when I speak to you through the essence of Saint Paul the Apostle on earth, Marie-Josée T.. For she is also a messenger of God, as I was during my earthly life as Joan of Arc. I am delighted to give her my dictations, to speak to her personally, to listen to her talk to me, and to impart courage and determination in her mission on earth.

For the mission of a messenger of God is always difficult, prone to misunderstanding as well as the persecution by men, and strewn with obstacles laid by the devil to prevent the conversion of souls to Christ Jesus.

Sufferings endured in the Name of Christ Jesus hold a cosmic value inestimable and unsuspected from the perspective of humans—but oh, so pleasant and sweet to the Eyes of the Eternal Father! For the imitation of Christ at all levels and in all dimensions prepares the way to redemption of the soul, the salvation so longed for by the faithful, such salvation being decided and allowed exclusively by God the Father Almighty, through His Son, the Saint Most High.

Alleluia! Alleluia! Alleluia! Blessed is Marie-Josée, who performs her mission in obedience and love of Christ Jesus our Savior. Amen. Alleluia!

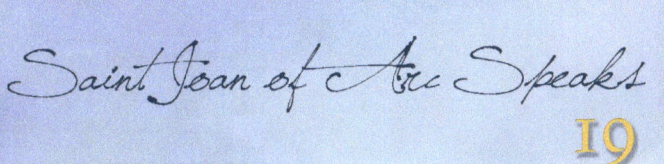

Saint Joan of Arc Speaks

y beloved children, I am delighted to get to know you through these transcendent ways, for when you are reading me, your soul is being magnetized more and more toward me. You are a Light for us, the inhabitants of Paradise, and your Light is unique to each one of you. Your Light, your inner Christ who dwells in your soul, varies in intensity according to your emotional and Spiritual states, and according to your psychological work.

In fact, when you are serene, in harmony with yourself and the Teachings of Christ Jesus, your unique Light is beautiful like a beautiful blue sun. When you are confused, anxious, frightened, and imprisoned in the ego, your unique Light is tarnished, soiled, and above all, obscured. Do you see? Your Light—your soul, your essence—is so important to us!

We hurry to you all, we rejoice over the progress made by the Lights that are flooded with Christic Energy. Though saddened, we remain attentive and devoted to the Lights that delay to convert to Christ Jesus.

Saint Joan of Arc Speaks

I love you. I am next to you and my presence with you intensifies in proportion to and commensurate with the prayers of intercession to my intention before God the Father. For the universe, created by God the Eternal Father, is conceived fundamentally of Energy, and the Law of attraction is everywhere applied therein. Consequently, the more you invoke me, the more I approach you. The more your Light shines like a beautiful blue sun, the more the Cosmic Christ fuses with your essence—with your soul—and makes it even more beautiful from here above. For the Love of Christ is the Light of the world.

Alleluia! Alleluia! Alleluia! I am Saint Joan of Arc and I love you! Amen. So be it.

Saint Joan of Arc Speaks

20

y dear children of the earth in peril, listen to me when I speak to you, whether here, through these Sacred Lines, or through the direct experience of my Presence in your Etheric Energy. For I speak to you, dear reader, more often than you might imagine.

Many spurs of inspiration that you have, moments of certainty, instances of faith and hope, are deliberately laid down in your heart by the Holy Spirit—God the Holy Spirit. For the Holy Spirit communicates to you the deep understanding of the Mysteries related to your Spiritual reality, the only reality that you need to concern yourself with. The Holy Spirit teaches you, the Holy Spirit enlightens you, the Holy Spirit guides you away from the circumstances of life wherein you risk falling or slowing down on your path of return to God.

Alleluia! Alleluia! Alleluia! Blessed are they who listen to me through the intervention of the Holy Spirit, for Miracles and Blessings are promised to them. Amen! Alleluia!

Saint Joan of Arc Speaks

y children, I pray for you continually. I pray for you and I love you with a Divine Love that is beyond your human understanding. Why look elsewhere for comfort and relief? I am here for you; the Saints in Paradise also are completely dedicated to you. Why are you ignoring the help from Heaven available to you immediately?

Verily, verily I say unto you, Heaven will come closer to earth, more and more so in times ahead, and you will witness more and more miracles around you. For such is the Desire of God the Father, the Father Almighty, Who decides everything, absolutely everything, taking place on earth.

Alleluia! Alleluia! Alleluia! Blessed are the believers in God, for God Himself will come into their lives! Amen. Alleluia!

For the imitation of Christ at all levels

and in all dimensions

prepares the way of
redemption of the soul,

the salvation so longed for
by the faithful!

Saint Joan of Arc Speaks

My children of the earth, I will appear on earth with my physical body preserved from 1431 among the darkness that will invade the earth. I will appear, and I will enlighten those who will have become close to me in the interim. I will appear in order to lead humans converted to Christ to victory against the enemy; for the enemy takes many forms, sometimes demonic, sometimes subtle and deceptive.

Anything that is not of Christ is the enemy and must be eliminated; and this, here and now, and when events start taking place.

Verily, verily I say unto you, be strong, be brave, as I teach you, because the struggle over human souls between the White Forces and the dark forces, occurring in dimensions other than you know, is an intense and continuous battle which will only intensify.

Alleluia! Alleluia! Alleluia! Let us pray together to the Eternal God that He bestows upon you now the Graces of Strength and Courage necessary for the battle against the dark forces. Amen. So be it.

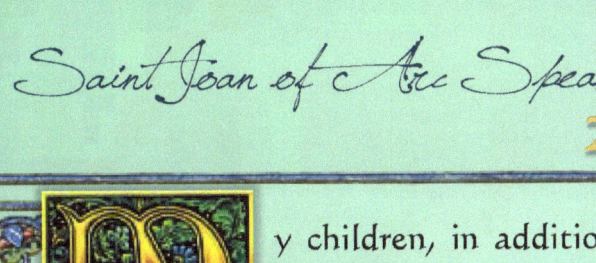

y children, in addition to appearing personally in the future to souls chosen by Christ Jesus, God the Father and myself, I shall be active in the military conflict that will be set in motion. I can hardly describe the atrocities of the war ahead…This is why we must pray now, today. Pray! Pray! Pray! So that you are spared the sight of the cruelties and horrors of war!

For this war will be more terrible and more demoniac than the wars that this humanity in distress has already experienced. Pray now, pray, and you will be rescued and saved!

Our Father who art in Heaven, hallowed be thy Name. Thy Kingdom come. Thy Will be done on earth as it is in Heaven. Give us this day our daily bread, and forgive us our trespasses, as we forgive those who trespass against us, and lead us not into temptation, but deliver us from evil. For Thine is the Kingdom, the Power, and the Glory, for ever and ever. Amen. Alleluia!

Saint Joan of Arc Speaks

24

My children of the earth, listen to me. Despite my upcoming Presence on earth, the battle will be difficult. The outcome has already been decided by God the Father Almighty: of course, the White Forces will earn victory over the dark forces. However, there will be many tears and much wailing, cries of despair and shouts for help, and this, across the entire earth. For the events that lie ahead will be terrible...

Alleluia! Alleluia! Alleluia! Blessed is he who prays today, and is preparing today, for the Justice of God will spare him. Amen! Alleluia!

Saint Joan of Arc Speaks

 listen to you during the prayers that you say before God the Father, Christ Jesus our King, and the Blessed Virgin Mary. Be firm and clear in your requests and petitions, be humble and contrite before the Trinity, direct your consciousness deeply into your heart, and experience a strong and sincere emotion during your prayers.

Much beyond listening to your prayers, the whole Heaven wishes to feel your prayers in order to attract the desired results! It is a fundamental Energetic issue that supplements the ultimate Decision made by God toward everything, absolutely everything, taking place on earth. You cannot take another breath unless God the Father has expressed this wish. For God the Father is everywhere, in everything, throughout everything, at all times, and nothing and no one can escape His Will.

Alleluia! Alleluia! Alleluia! Blessed is he who loves God and fears God, as this is a sound approach of a humble and contrite heart before God the Father. Amen. So be it.

Saint Joan of Arc Speaks

26

y children, my children: love one another and forgive. More than ever, this teaching of Christ Jesus is wonderful and critical for the salvation of your soul! Do not delay putting into action this fundamental Teaching of Christ Jesus among those around you.

*L*ove, no matter the mistakes and imperfections of others! Forgive, despite the seriousness of the insolence committed against you! For God the Father is very sensitive to souls who imitate His Only Son, our Lord Jesus Christ, in all aspects, from His Teaching of Love to His Teaching of Suffering on the Cross!

I repeat: love one another and forgive—and you will please God our Father! Amen! Alleluia!

✥ † † † † † ✥

Saint Joan of Arc Speaks

27

My friends, be gentle and attentive to all those around you, the same way that you would be gentle and attentive if Jesus Christ walked with you... For in fact, He walks with you!

Christ Jesus, in His Universal and Cosmic nature, inhabits all hearts in the whole world, regardless of their degrees of devotion to Him! This is why the Teaching reveals that what you do to your fellowman, you do also to Christ Jesus. For this is true. Hence become, my friends, my children, in a state of awakening and of special consideration for each and every one, honoring Christ Jesus Who dwells in each one of you.

Alleluia! Alleluia! Alleluia! Blessed is he who sees Christ and who blesses Christ in each one of you. Amen. So be it.

Saint Joan of Arc Speaks

 y dear children, hasten to join the Legion of Saint Paul! For this Legion has obtained from God the Father a very particular Divine Mercy. The emblematic five crosses are very Powerful in the Eyes of God the Father and He allows accordingly accelerated redemption to these souls. For members of the Legion of Saint Paul are blessed by the Holy Trinity and their mission is written in God the Eternal Father's Plan of Salvation.

My sword, the one I found in a church, was also marked by the five crosses. This miraculous and merciful sword for my soul had been placed at this location by the Angels of Christ Himself. At the very beginning of my mission, I did not know the cosmic meaning of the five crosses; this Mystery was taught to me in Heaven.

Alleluia! Alleluia! Alleluia! Blessed are the members of the Legion of Saint Paul, for the Kingdom of Heaven is theirs! Amen!

Saint Joan of Arc Speaks

y children of the promised earth, I bless you in the Name of the Father, and of the Son, and of the Holy Spirit. I became a Christ, at the image of Christ Jesus crucified for us, and as a result, I am among the Saints in Paradise, who are able to perform miracles for you.

All the Saints are also Christ, for they have absorbed the Christic Energy in a Total and Eternal manner during their journey on earth. They followed the Teaching of Christ to the letter. They loved and forgave all, they suffered persecution and rejection as Christ did, and they demonstrated to God the Father an exemplary and flawless obedience. In short, they became Christ by the imitation of Christ at all levels.

Your life will also be focused on Christ very soon because of profound changes brought about in you right now. For this miraculous book that you are holding in your hands is truly a Magnetic Force that attracts the Benefactors of Heaven to your side in order to accelerate the process of purification of your soul. For your salvation at the moment of passage that is death depends upon the purity of your soul.

Saint Joan of Arc Speaks

Alleluia! Alleluia! Alleluia! Let us pray together Christ Jesus, Christ Most High, our Master and our Only Model of unsurpassed Cosmic Perfection. Amen. Alleluia!

My Jesus, my Savior

84

Saint Joan of Arc Speaks

30

y dear children, be joyful and glad for Heaven has opened up for your salvation! My Voice is heard among you...finally! It has been so long that I wanted to speak to you! Thank you, Marie-Josée, my beautiful soul, for writing my Words with so much love and obedience!

Alleluia! Alleluia! Alleluia! Blessed is he who comes in the Name of the Lord! Amen! Alleluia!

Saint Joan of Arc Speaks

31

 My children, pray now, for tomorrow is reserved for God, and God Himself decides everything, absolutely everything, at all times, taking place in your life. Pray to pay for the mistakes committed in the past, pray so to obtain the Graces of understanding the Mysteries of Heaven, pray for Mercy on your soul and those whom you hold in your heart, pray for the salvation of humanity. Pray! Pray! Pray!

Have God the Father listen to your inner voice—your child's voice, pure and sincere, dedicated and confident. Pray! Pray! Pray! From this moment on!

Holy, Holy, Holy Lord God of Hosts. Heaven and earth are full of Your Glory: Hosanna in the Highest. Blessed is he who comes in the Name of the Lord: Hosanna in the Highest. Amen.

Saint Joan of Arc Speaks

My dear children of the earth, I would like to share with you some aspects of my life that you do not know.

First: Clothing. Yes, I chose to wear men's clothes because the political and military climate of the time did not permit the display of regular female attributes. I received specific instructions about this from the Saints and Angels who guided me. I was told that wearing men's clothes was not only more appropriate to perform the task that awaited me, but would serve as an example of strength and courage, and especially of rebellion, for generations to follow.

For every battle is a form of rebellion against the perverse and satanic forces who wish to take dominion over the earth. We must say No to temptation; we must recover, and prepare to go to battle with the attributes of courage and tenacity that are applicable to the arising situation.

Alleluia! Alleluia! Alleluia! Blessed are the hearts that are willing to go to battle, for I, Saint Joan of Arc, will be there with them in combat. Amen. Alleluia.

Saint Joan of Arc Speaks

My children, my children, listen to me well: many things have been written about me that are wrong.

I wish to clarify here that none of the members of my family were killed or wounded during the few attacks that my village suffered during my childhood. My family and I had always left my village just in time and so we were able to avoid danger. I am thankful to our Lord Jesus Christ our Savior.

Also, let me say that I did not know how to ride a horse when I joined the army of the king. My ease at mounting a horse was of supernatural origin. This Gift was bestowed upon me by God Himself so to allow me to best conduct my mission. I give thanks to God the Father for so much Love toward me.

Also, let me specify that I was not a bastard. I am the legitimate child of my father, Jacques d'Arc, and my mother Isabelle. May this error be dispelled once and for all; I make this my prayer through this miraculous book of truth.

Alleluia! Alleluia! Alleluia! Let the truth be proclaimed about the life of Saint Joan of Arc through Heaven opening up to you by virtue of this book blessed by God! Amen. Alleluia!

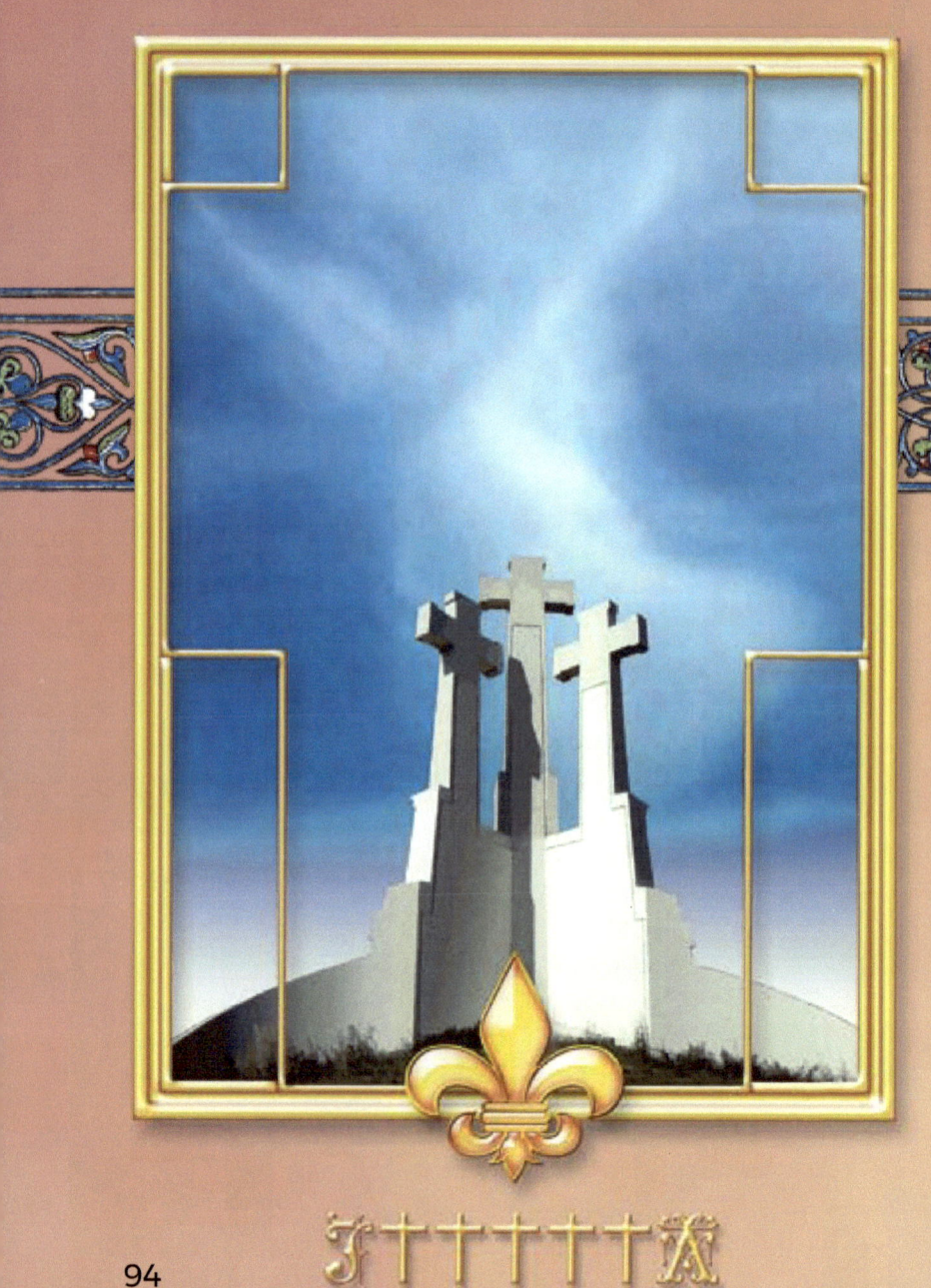

Saint Joan of Arc Speaks

34

My beloved children, always remain in the faith and hope in Christ Jesus. Nothing happening to you is the result of chance, nothing that has preceded in your life and nothing in your future. The Energy of Christ is the very nature of all life and of events taking place in it.

I love you in the Name of the Father, and of the Son, and of the Holy Spirit. Amen. Alleluia!

Saint Joan of Arc Speaks

35

y beloved children of the earth, listen to me carefully. The secret that I shared with king Charles VII when I met him for the first time was the revelation of a message coming directly from God the Father. This Divine revelation made by God Himself to Charles shook him deeply and allowed him to trust me completely. The content of this message will be revealed in the future to my readers of the following tome.

For now, I want you to understand that this secret originating from Heaven had nothing to do with an alleged common family heredity or anything with regard to my person—that is to say, Joan. Let this be very clear.

Alleluia! Alleluia! Alleluia! May the Holy Life of Christ beat in your heart always, for ever and ever! Amen. Alleluia!

Saint Joan of Arc Speaks

y children of the enchanted earth, I hasten to tell you today that I love you. My Love for you is of Christic and Divine nature and cannot be measured at the emotional level that you know.

When I was on earth, wearing men's clothes at the forefront of the military battle, my love for France and the French was an important motivation for my behavior—in addition to my love for Christ Jesus, my Lord and my God, primordial and determinant love within all my actions.

Today, as I navigate through the Etheric dimensions as I wish, by virtue of my body having been preserved from fire in 1431 by Christ Jesus my Savior, I want to tell you that I love you madly, I love you wildly, I love you passionately, for I have become Love, as Christ Jesus our Master.

I love you and I will always love you, no matter your interest with regard to my influence in your life. I love you and wish to teach you that the Eternal Father loves you with an Ineffable and Transcendent Love that challenges human comprehension. I love you and wish to convey to you the love for your own mission, carefully and lovingly chosen for each one of you by the Eternal Father.

Saint Joan of Arc Speaks
Tome I

This mission, this life plan, always implies strength and courage; this is why I am intervening in your life at this moment of your journey on earth. For I am the Queen of Angels who labor for your victory against the obstacles of life.

Alleluia! Alleluia! Alleluia! Blessed is he who lets himself be loved by me, Saint Joan of Arc, Queen of Strength and Courage and Queen of Angels surrounding you. Amen. Alleluia!

Thy Peace On Earth Must Be Achieved
†

No Light Nor Litany
Must Be Spared
To Honor Thy Grace

Saint Joan of Arc Speaks

38

y children, I love you and I will guide you to victory. Death to Spiritual laziness! Death to idleness of all kinds! Death to delay! Death to denial! Death to everything that is an obstacle on your way to God the Father, hand in hand with Christ Jesus, accompanied by the Saints in Paradise and the Angels of God!

I say unto you, I say unto you verily, the battle will be difficult; however, the help we are offering from here above is guaranteed to give you victory. Say Yes now! Wield your sword of faith in Christ Jesus! Take a breath full of strength and courage! Raise your head straight up, smile, and behold God the Father with love, with gratitude and with hope!

I am there. I will always be there to guide you, inspire you, comfort you—the same way that Saint Catherine, Saint Margaret, and Saint Michael the Archangel came forward during my earthly life.

Saint Joan of Arc Speaks
Tome I

I promise my direct intervention in your life according to your level of sincerity, of dedication, and of prayer to God, linked to my intercession. According to the Law of attraction that exists in the temporal world that is yours, our attraction is fundamentally magnetic and authentic. The more you come to me, the more I come to you.... Pray! Pray! Pray! And the Celestial visitations will begin! Amen!

Alleluia! Alleluia! Alleluia! Blessed are the prayerful before God, for He sends His messengers as He pleases as a reward for the virtue of hope! Amen. So be it.

Saint Joan of Arc Speaks

y dear children of the earth, I hasten to tell you a story. When I was a child, I lived in a small village, simple and poorly-known (the village has become very popular after my death). One day, as I was walking in the woods all alone, I saw a man in his thirties, wearing a white dress. I thought his skin was tanned, but in fact, his skin was golden color. I was not frightened; on the contrary, I was attracted by this beautiful man I had never seen before and who was not part of my village!

As I walked toward him, curious, he said: "Come, my child." His voice was sweeter than honey, more captivating than the warm rays of the sun. I walked a little closer, joyfully and carefully, and all of a sudden, I felt transported at high speed into another dimension, in the midst of Holy and Angelic figures who were smiling at me. And just as quickly as this vision appeared to me, it was gone, and I found myself lying on my back in the tall grass where I had walked!

Saint Joan of Arc Speaks

I knew then that I had met Christ Jesus, our Savior, and He made me travel for an instant. And I visited Paradise with Him! This vision of Paradise, though never recorded by historians (due to the simple fact that I had never told anyone) supported me and comforted me in the many tribulations that followed. I am thankful to the Master Jesus for His compassion on my soul, which was preparing itself for such suffering as a messenger of God.

I say unto you, I say unto you verily, the Lord will always be there to assist you in your mission. Have no fear whatsoever.

*A*lleluia! Alleluia! Alleluia! Blessed is he who comes in the Name of the Lord! Amen! Alleluia!

Saint Joan of Arc Speaks

40

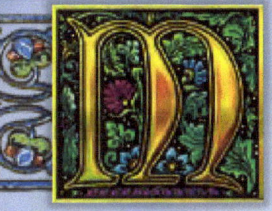y children, I am here and I speak to you within your heart. Listen to me through these miraculous Words written on this page and listen to me in the conversations I have with you in the depths of your heart.

I say unto you, I say unto you verily, I establish with you, by the intermediary of this book originating from Heaven and from your heart itself, and with the Supreme Permission of the Absolute Father—I establish with you therefore a Tangible, Sacred, and Cosmic Connection that will last for Eternity. For my Holiness has entered your life by virtue of this powerful book, and cannot leave you, regardless of your will.

The Words you are reading are my Words, the Words of Saint Joan of Arc, and my Words are Sources of Strength and Courage in your life. These virtues of strength and courage are of a Transcendent and Divine quality that goes beyond what the human imagination can conceive.

Saint Joan of Arc Speaks

The source of strength and courage I infuse in your life derives from the Source of Life itself, the Christic Source of Jesus, our Savior. Every Saint in Paradise fulfills a special function here; thus, my virtue is linked to the merits of the brave heart that gives itself to the battle on behalf of Jesus the Christ—the battle for souls.

Alleluia! Alleluia! Alleluia! Blessed are the hearts receiving me, for my Holy Strength and my Holy Courage accompany them always and for Eternity! Amen. So be it.

Saint Joan of Arc Speaks

y children, I love you with an Infinite Love, transcendent and magnificent, more beautiful than all the dreams of men assembled together. I love you and I will always love you, until the end of time—and beyond. As Saint Paul the Apostle, from now on, I will intervene in your life in order to correct your laziness and your indifference with regards to your Spiritual reality and the urgent situation that you must confront soon.

I love you and I want you to know that my Love for you cannot fluctuate or weaken because of your mistakes or your offenses. Being Christ myself, like all the Saints in Paradise, I have absorbed the Universal Teaching that is Divine Love, and henceforth, it is my turn to teach it to you.

Your life will never be the same: your steps will be decisive, your emotions will be positive, your mind will be fluid and charitable, your will shall be strong and courageous: that is my Cosmic Signature, imbued herein.

Alleluia! Alleluia! Alleluia! Blessed be your life, dear reader, for your life has been carefully chosen by here above in order to receive Divine Love and to experience Divine Love! Amen! So be it.

Saint Joan of Arc Speaks

My children, remain in peace and gladness, for God our Father has had Mercy upon your soul, by virtue of this miraculous book that you are holding in your hands. I, Saint Joan of Arc, by virtue of the magnetic connection that is established here, at this moment, have been assigned to take care of your soul: to make it strong and courageous.

I wish and I ensure that your soul acquires the Divine attributes of Strength and Courage— ineffable virtues that transcend all human qualities, even the highest. Consequently, the Strength and Courage of a Divine nature that I communicate to you through my very Holiness cannot be found elsewhere on earth.

Saint Joan of Arc Speaks

Verily, verily I say unto you, events that are fast approaching will require defensive attributes of Divine Origin to ensure survival. No quality of human origin whatsoever will be great enough to allow you to sustain life, unless there is intervention of Divine Providence. For only matter in harmony with Christic vibrations (or very close to Christ) will be able to withstand the transition ahead.

Alleluia! Alleluia! Alleluia! Blessed are those who read these Lines, for Divine Strength and Divine Courage are communicated to them at this time by Saint Joan of Arc Herself. Amen. So be it.

Let us give Glory to God for such Mercy. Amen. Alleluia!

Saint Joan of Arc Speaks

43

y children, may you be able to hear me like the essence of Saint Paul, Marie-Josée T. Her gift of clairaudience and clairvoyance allows her to hear me and see me in the Celestial Court surrounding her. I make my prayer that all who read me may one day hear me and see me the same way! Amen! Alleluia!

Saint Joan of Arc Speaks

44

y dear children of the earth, guard your thoughts and your emotions. Always be vigilant with regards to the psychological elements invading you. Be prepared to reject what is harmful and negative, that which is unnecessary and unproductive and that derives from the manipulation of the ego and that originates, in fact, from an evil source.

You must constantly monitor the psychological environment in which you live inside you, making sure everything is always of Spiritual origin, oriented toward Charity, overflowing with Love, raised to Mercy, blessed in the Grace of God the Father, walking with Christ Jesus, our Savior to all.

For you are responsible for your own psychological states, through the power of your will—not us, not Christ Jesus, or even God the Father. You must choose between Light and darkness in your inner world by yourself, consenting to one thing or the other by virtue of your freedom of choice, granted by the Father.

Saint Joan of Arc Speaks

Merits and Glory in Heaven with us await you if you agree to the Light, moment by moment, in your life. Fears and torments await you, in your life and after the transition which is death, if you opt for the forces opposed to the Light, to Love, to Charity. For you are deciding today about your future life, based on your current decisions.

Alleluia! Alleluia! Alleluia! Blessed is he who walks in the Light today, as Light shall increase, for ever and ever. Amen. Alleluia.

My beloved children of the earth, rejoice and be glad, for the events ahead will soon make way for a New Sun. The contradictions of this world of chaos shall be no longer, just as perversity and cruelty committed against men and against Christ.

Alleluia! Alleluia! Alleluia! Blessed are they whom Providence leads to the New Sun! Amen!

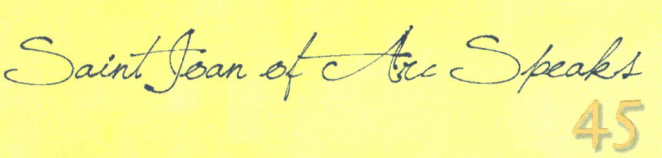
Saint Joan of Arc Speaks

y children, my children, I embrace you and I will keep you under my Protection, Holy and Divine. I will never abandon you. Rejoice and be glad in your heart for you have met me through this blessed book!

Call for me, invoke me, ask for my intercession before God the Father to obtain anything—several times a day. The Miracles I will perform in your life are limitless and will shower you with unparalleled Graces. You will be enchanted and marveled by the power of prayer recited with the intercession of the Saints in Paradise!

I bless you in the Name of the Father, and of the Son, and of the Holy Spirit.

Other Messages on my part will follow very shortly.

I love you so much.

Jeanne
Saint Joan of Arc.

Afterword

Perhaps the best way to describe Joan's visitations is to liken her to an extra layer of yourself. She can enhance your thoughts, emotions, and motivations for the better. Going up a flight of stairs with Joan of Arc and without Joan of Arc are not the same.

She has beautiful long reddish hair, a stunning graceful face with gorgeous blue eyes, and is clad in glorious silvery armor.

My life is so unique—I wake up each morning and find Joan standing next to me! She quickly gets me out of bed and starts chatting away, recapping the events of the prior day, envisioning the day ahead, and making and changing plans as I go through my morning routine, which involves eating breakfast, getting dressed, and putting my makeup on. We even have girl-to-girl locker room conversations all the time.

Most importantly, she sits down next to me when I pray to God. Praying to God without Joan of Arc feels so different: I know God the Father Almighty delights in our joined prayers.

Find out how Joan can do the same for you; invite Joan of Arc into your life!

Joan, I love you!

Marie-Josée

About the author

Marie-Josée Thibault's life is in no way similar to yours. When she wakes, the saints of Heaven visit her, talk to her, teach her, and pray intensely with her. When such mystical sessions draw to a close, she greets with great respect and deep reverence the Masters of the Heavenly Court. This servant of the Lord spends the rest of the day in the company of her guardian angel, who continues her spiritual education and ceaselessly protects her from the perils of this fallen world.

Bestowed by the Heavenly Father, her gifts of clairvoyance and clairaudience allow her to remain in continuous contact with the supernatural dimension juxtaposed with ours, where the soul is born of the Spirit through Jesus and Mary. She prays that, one day soon, the entire human race will give glory to the Father, the Son, and the Holy Spirit.

Also by author

- Saint Padre Pio Speaks: Book 1
- Abba, Your Father, Speaks: Book I
- Abba, Your Father, Speaks: Book II
- Angel Gabriel Speaks: Book 1
- Saint Beethoven Speaks: Book 1
- Saint Bernadette Speaks Book 1
- Dear Humanity: Book 1
- Dear Humanity: Book 2
- Saint Therese of Lisieux Speaks: Book 1

FREE DOWNLOAD

Get your free copy of :
"Saint Padre Pio Speaks: Book 1"
when you sign up to the
author's VIP mailing list!
Get started here:

www.abbamyfatheriloveyou.com